SOUNDS THAT BREAK THE SILENCE

SOUNDS THAT BREAK THE SILENCE

Compiled by
MARIAN PORTEL
with an introduction
by
JAMES X. WILLIAMS

STANYAN BOOKS

RANDOM HOUSE

A Stanyan Book
Published by Stanyan Books,
8721 Sunset Blvd.,
Hollywood, California 90069
and by Random House, Inc.
201 East 50th Street,
New York, N.Y. 10022

**Library of Congress Catalogue
Card Number: 73-8009**

ISBN: 0-394-48599-8

Printed in U.S.A.

Illustrations by Frank Bender
Designed by Hy Fujita

First Printing

Introduction

In *Sounds That Break the Silence*
Marian Portel has compiled a book
that holds out a hand of hope to
people of all ages and faiths.

While it deals with love and courage
and brotherhood and both tender and
trying times, its keynote is the trite but
true message—of which we all need
to be reminded—that life is beautiful.

In my opinion, this small volume is a
font of inspiration for everyone,
affirming as it does the wonder of
humanity and nature and God.

— James X. Williams

We all had a girl
and her name was Nostalgia.

— **Ernest Hemingway**

Every shadow points to the sun.

— **Ralph W. Emerson**

The most important things in life
aren't things.

— **Kathryn Maye**

I picked a bulldog for my kids so
they'd see that ugly face and
discover all this love behind it —
and never take anything
at face value.

— **Flip Wilson**

I'm naturally sad. Time and everything else makes one reflective. Happiness is a negative thing; I think the emotion thing is more important than happiness.

— **Charlie Chaplin**

I once had a sparrow alight on my shoulder while hoeing in a village garden, and I felt I was more distinguished by that circumstance than I should have been by any epaulet I could have worn.

— **Henry D. Thoreau**

Four ducks on a pond,
A grass bank beyond,
A blue sky of spring,
White clouds on the wing;
What a little thing
To remember for years—
To remember with tears!

— **William Allingham**

There's no point to feeling sorry for
yourself, or else you want to go
and die by the side of the road.
Some day that will happen,
but there's no point in making it
happen sooner rather than later.

— **An anonymous sharecropper**

I know it's not so good for us,
but there's never a day I don't
see something I like.

— **A child of the above
sharecropper**

Life is too short to be little.

— Benjamin Disraeli

Love looks through a telescope;
envy through a microscope.

— Josh Billings

Happiness consists of a great love
and much serving.

— Dr. Louisa Duffe Booth

'Rejoice with them that rejoice.'
Little thing as this seems,
it still is extremely great, and
requireth the spirit of true wisdom.

— St. Augustine

No man is hurt but by himself.

— Diogenes

God is my banker.
I may not have everything I want
but I have everything I need.

— Ethel Waters

If God were not a necessary being
of himself, he might almost seem
to be made for the use and
benefit of man.

— John Tillotson

What things soever ye desire,
when ye pray, believe that ye
receive them,
and ye shall have them.

— Mark 11:24

The splitting apart of man from man
dooms more than splitting the
atom can.

— Louis Ginsberg

Somehow we all must learn to
know one another.

— Robert Coles

Never yet was a springtime,
Late though lingered the snow,
That the sap stirred not
   at the whisper
Of the southwind, sweet and low;
Never yet was a springtime
When the buds forgot to blow.

       — **Margaret E. Sangster**

The birds are moulting.
If only man could moult also —
his mind once a year its errors,
his heart once a year its
useless passions.

— James Lane Allen

I believe I'm turned around now.
It started with the police who
arrested me. I saw they were
human beings. I used to be angry
at all police. Now I can't thank them
enough . . . I need to get involved
in the real world, not the
make-believe world. I never really
considered what freedom was until
I lost mine. I never really
understood what democracy was
until I lost my freedom.

— "Douglas"
A prisoner at Attica

We have no right to ask when sorrow comes, "Why did this happen to me?" unless we ask the same question for every joy that comes our way.

— **Philip S. Bernstein**

The way to love anything is to realize that it might be lost.

— **G. K. Chesterton**

The soft sound of empty is the next voice you will hear.

— **Rod McKuen**

Adversity attracts the man of character. He seeks out the bitter joy of responsibility.

— Charles de Gaulle

A good laugh
is sunshine in a house.

— **William M. Thackeray**

A light heart lives long.

— Bessie Lorraine Boles

There is nothing in the world so irresistibly contagious as laughter and good humour.

— Charles Dickens

Nothing's harder on your laurels than resting on them.

— Franklin P. Jones

When, following the 1971 World Series final game the Pirates' Roberto Clemente was praised before TV cameras, he asked to say a few words to his parents.
In Spanish he said,
"On this, the proudest moment of my life, I ask your blessing."

Instructions regarding his burial crypt
at a New England school for
retarded children:

Make it simple, no ornamentation.
And make it so I'm facing the
school, so I can always be looking
at the children.

— Richard Cardinal Cushing

I'm Nobody! Who are you?
Are you — Nobody — too?

— Emily Dickinson

Ever since I began singing in the
big concert halls, people have been
trying to teach me to be grand,
but I just can't do it.

— **Mahalia Jackson**

My mother doesn't ask for a fur or a
diamond or a car, like all the other
women in my life do. And it
reminds me that poverty is pure.

— **Marcello Mastroianni**

I know I am—that simplest bliss
That millions of my brothers miss.

— **Bayard Taylor**

I wanted to be a blonde.
My ambition was first to be a
cheerleader and then an airline
stewardess — like the average girl.
Then I realized that as the average
girl I was a failure.
So I decided to be myself.

— Buffy Sainte-Marie

Black Americans can give service
to their own people and to Africa
instead of rhetoric. They have an
access to knowledge and training
that is the envy of most black people
everywhere in the world.
All they have to do (besides work
hard) is to let down their buckets
where they are.

— Roy Wilkins

Fill a house with animals,
and you fill it with love.

— Hubert De Givenchy

When I was 22 I had this whole
world staring me in the face.
I didn't know what I was going to do
and I didn't have the security.
I realized then that's the definition
of being alive:
Being alive is being vulnerable.

— **Hugh Downs**

If mankind had wished for what is
right, they might have had it
long ago.

— **William Hazlitt**

When life is true to the poles
of nature, the streams of truth will
roll through us in song.

— **Ralph W. Emerson**

The Net Natural Environment is
more important than the Gross
National Product.
We've got to think about God
and not materialism.

— **Walter J. Hickel**

How can any man watch a sunset
and be sad?

— **Bela Lugosi**

Happy the man whose wish and
    care
      A few paternal acres bound,
Content to breath his native air
    In his own ground.

Whose herds with milk,
    whose fields with bread,
Whose flocks supply him with
    attire,
Whose trees in summer yield him
    shade,
      In winter, fire.

— Alexander Pope

One cannot always be a hero
but one can always be a man.

— Goethe

A religion without mystery
must be a religion without God.

— Jeremy Taylor

We hold upon this earth the
place of Almighty God.

— Pope Leo XIII

All I have seen teaches me to trust
the Creator for all I have not seen.

— Ralph W. Emerson

We expect too much of God,
but he always seems ready.

— John F. Kennedy

Live among men as if God beheld
you; speak with God as if men
were listening.

— Seneca

Whoever falls from God's right
hand is caught in his left.

— Edwin Markham

If money is inadequate to improve education, the residents of poor districts should at least have an equal opportunity to be disappointed by its failure.

— **John E. Coons**

It's sweet pain because, however they try to hurt me, I know that just by sticking it out I'm going to help end the whole system of segregation; and that can make you go through anything.

— **A black student in a white school**

If it's too heavy to move,
too hard to chop and too green
to burn, just plow around it.

— **Abraham Lincoln**

I'm tired of hearing it said that
democracy doesn't work.
Of course it doesn't work.
It isn't supposed to work.
We are supposed to work it.

— **Alexander Woollcott**

All great discoveries are made by
men whose feelings run ahead of
their thinking.

— Charles Parkhurst

All great art is the expression of
man's delight in God's work,
not his own.

— **John Ruskin**

I want to make something so big
that nobody can possess it.

— **Claes Oldenburg**

Three passions, simple but
unsurmountably strong, have
governed my life—a longing for
love, a yearning for knowledge,
and an unbearable pity
for the suffering of mankind.

— Bertrand Russell

There is nothing so powerful
as truth — and often nothing
so strange.

—Daniel Webster

The sounds that break the
silence are the ones you
never hear.

— Rod McKuen

If the world's a vale of tears,
Smile til rainbows span it.
Breathe the love that life endears,
Clear of clouds, to fan it.

— Elmira Jules

There is nothing I can give you
which you have not;
But there is much, very much,
that while I cannot give it,
you can take.

No heaven can come to us unless
our hearts find rest in today.
Take heaven!
No peace lies in the future
which is not hidden in this
present instant.
Take peace!

— **fra Giovanni, 1513 A.D.**

I launched the phrase "The war to
end all war"— and that was not
the least of my crimes.

— H. G. Wells

Laws are silent in the midst of arms.

— Cicero

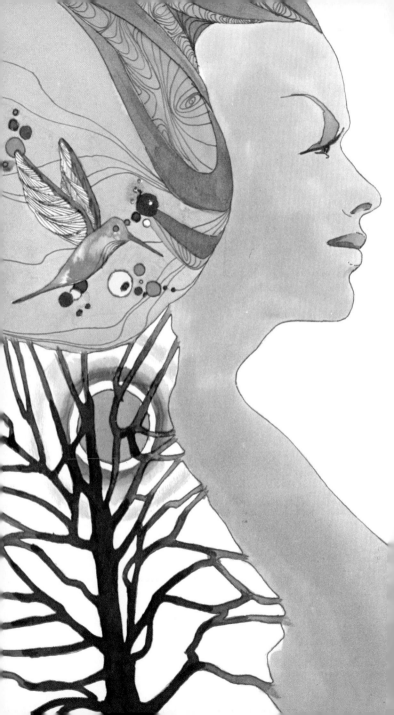

As we are not living in an
eternity, the time to be happy
is today.

— **Grenville Kleiser**

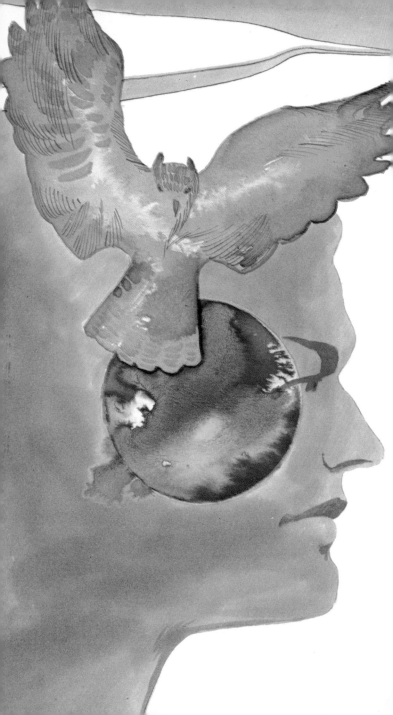

Courage is grace under pressure.

— Ernest Hemingway

The man who has least fear for
his own carcass has most time
to consider others.

— Robert L. Stevenson

All brave men love; for only
he is brave who has affections
to fight for.

— Nathaniel Hawthorne

Love consists in this—that
two solitudes protect and
touch and greet each other.

— Rainer Maria Rilke

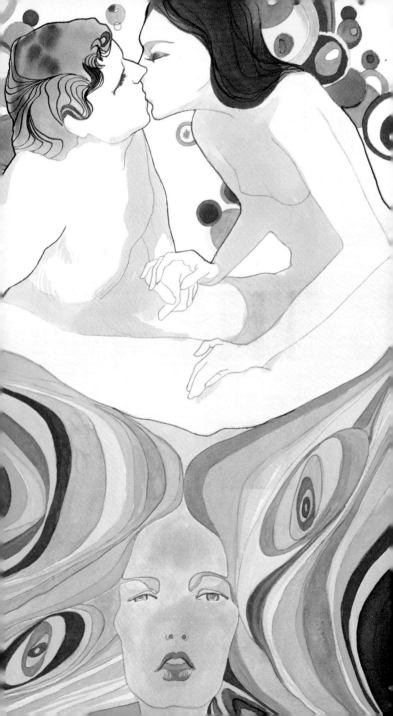